JUST VOICES

A CAPPELLA ANTHEMS FOR ANY

Compiled by Joseph M. Mar...
Featuring the Writers of Shawne...

T0078536

CONTENTS

GlorySound
A Division of Shawnee Press, Inc.
1221 17th Ave. South, Nashville TN 37212

Visit Shawnee Press Online at www.shawneepress.com

WOKE UP THIS MORNING

for S.A.T.B. voices, a cappella*

Traditional Spiritual

Arranged by
PATSY FORD SIMMS (ASCAP)

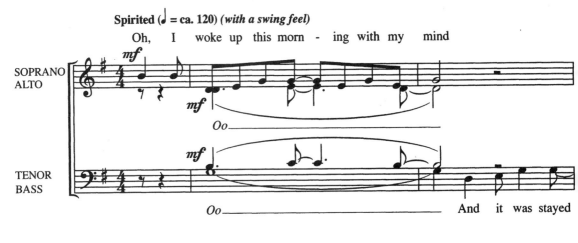

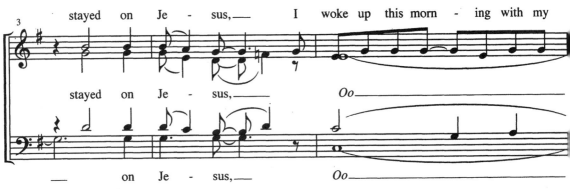

9 woke up this morn - ing with my mind

Oo _____ stayed on

Oo _____ And it was stayed __ on

12 Je - sus. __ Hal - le - lu, ___ hal - le - lu, ___ hal - le - lu - jah. __

Je - sus. __ Hal - le, hal - le - lu, __ hal - le - lu - jah. __

17

16 Oh, you can't hate your neigh - bor in your mind,

— Oo _____

— Oo _____ When you keep it stayed

19 stayed on Je - sus, __ You can't hate your neigh - bor in your

stayed on Je - sus, __ Oo _____

— on Je - sus, __ Oo _____

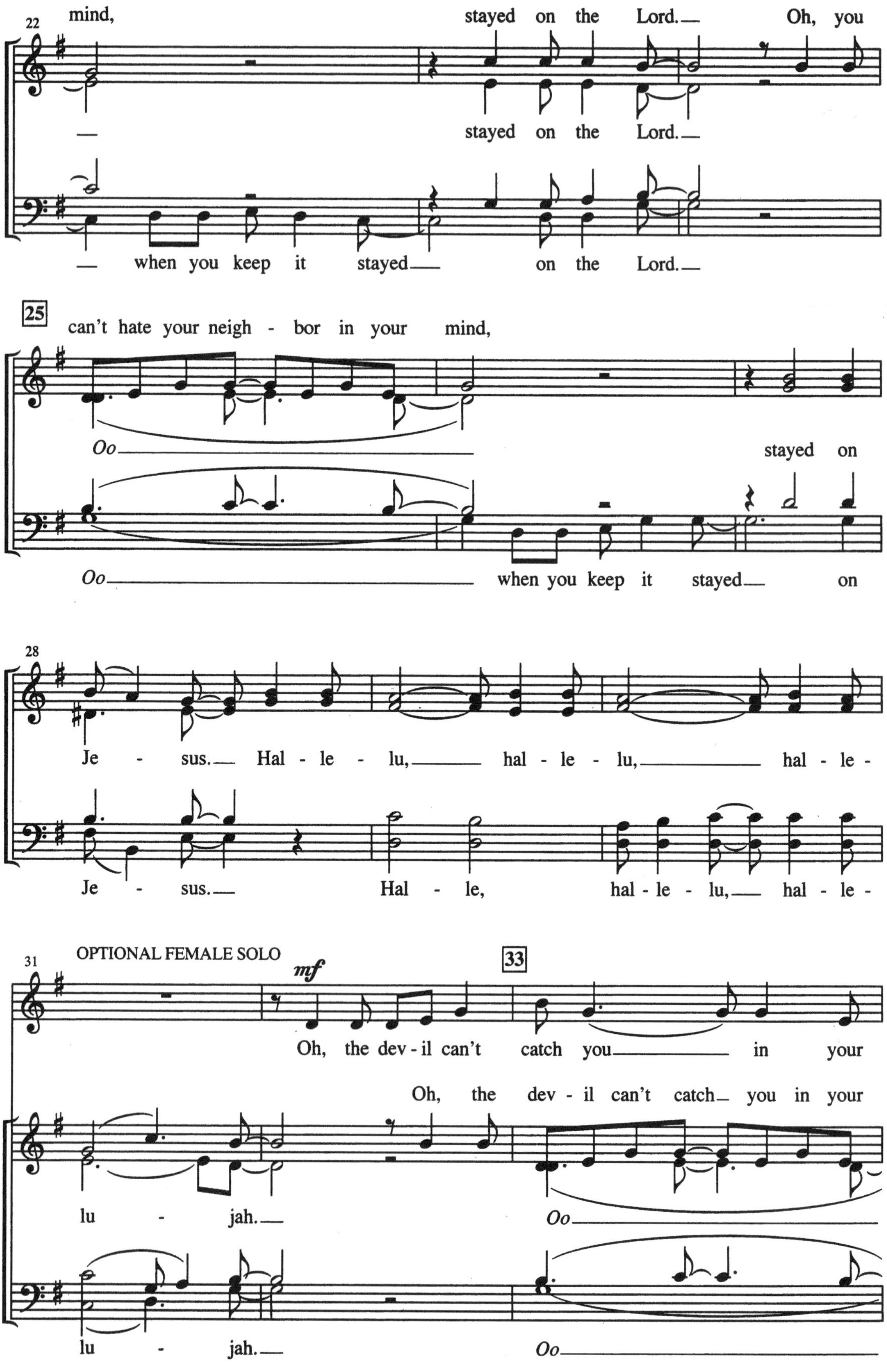
22
mind, stayed on the Lord. Oh, you
stayed on the Lord.
when you keep it stayed on the Lord.
25
can't hate your neigh - bor in your mind,
Oo
stayed on
Oo
when you keep it stayed on
28
Je - sus. Hal - le - lu, hal - le - lu, hal - le -
Je - sus. Hal - le, hal - le - lu, hal - le -
31
OPTIONAL FEMALE SOLO
mf
33
Oh, the dev - il can't catch you in your
Oh, the dev - il can't catch you in your
lu - jah.
Oo
lu - jah.
Oo

mind when you keep it on Je - sus, on Je - sus.—

mind, _____ stayed on Je - sus.— Hal - le -

_____ when you keep it stayed_____ on Je - sus.—

Hal - le - lu, hal - le - lu, hal - le - lu - jah.—

lu,_____ hal - le - lu,_____ hal - le - lu - jah.—

Hal - le, hal - le - lu,— hal - le - lu - jah.—

OPTIONAL MALE SOLO

_____ God's love will be with you_____ in your mind,

All · God's love will be with— you in your

_____ Oo—

_____ Oo—

keep it stayed,— keep it stayed on Je - sus.— God's

mind, stayed on Je - sus.— God's

— stayed on Je - sus.—

— if you keep it stayed— on Je - sus.—

love will be in your mind,— just keep it stayed on the Lord.

love will be with— you in your mind, stayed on the Lord.

Oo———————— stayed on the Lord.

Oo———————— if you keep it stayed— on the Lord.

— God's love will be with you———— in your mind,

— All God's love will be with— you in your

— Oo————

— Oo————

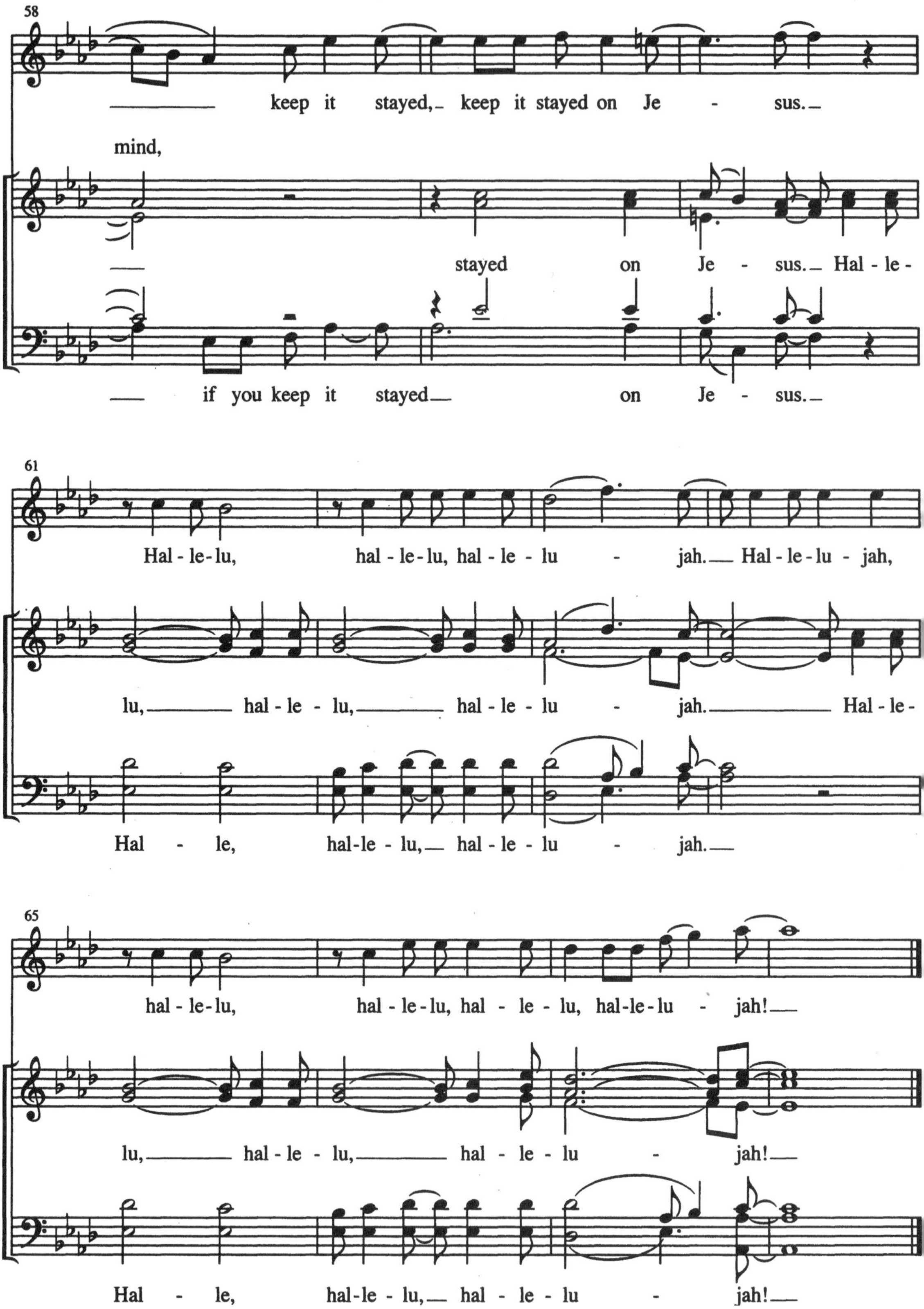
58
keep it stayed, keep it stayed on Je - sus.
mind,
stayed on Je - sus. Hal - le -
if you keep it stayed on Je - sus.
61
Hal - le-lu, hal - le-lu, hal - le - lu - jah. Hal - le - lu - jah,
lu, hal - le - lu, hal - le - lu - jah. Hal - le -
Hal - le, hal-le - lu, hal - le - lu - jah.
65
hal - le-lu, hal - le-lu, hal - le - lu, hal-le-lu - jah!
lu, hal - le - lu, hal - le - lu - jah!
Hal - le, hal-le - lu, hal - le - lu - jah!

DEEP RIVER

for S.A.T.B. voices, unaccompanied

Arranged by
ROY RINGWALD

TRADITIONAL SPIRITUAL

12

*A few sopranos hum the small notes.

DOWN TO THE WATER TO PRAY
(DOWN IN THE RIVER TO PRAY)

for S.A.T.B. voices, a cappella

Traditional
Additional lyrics by P.C.

Traditional
Arranged by
PEPPER CHOPLIN (ASCAP)

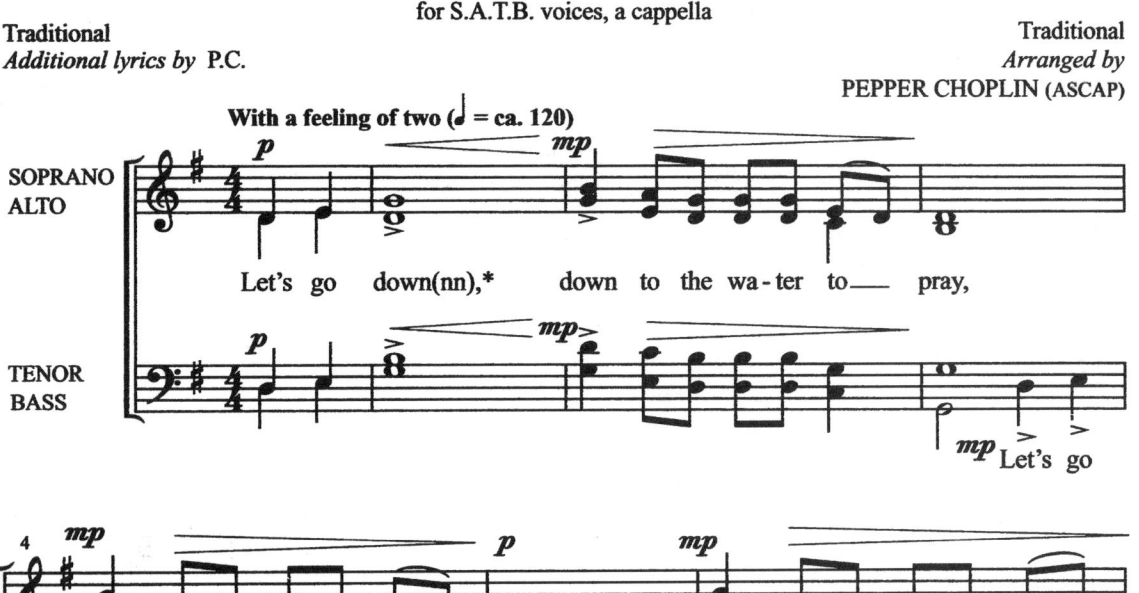

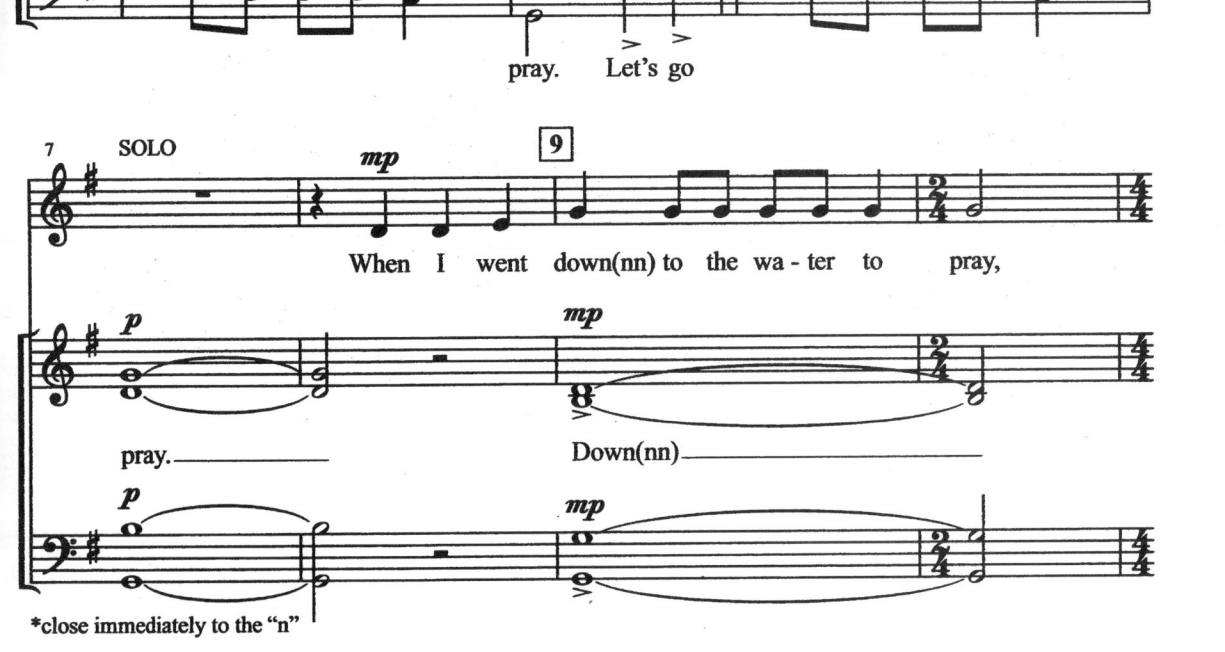

*close immediately to the "n"

14

Dedicated to the Choir of the United Presbyterian Church of St. Andrew, Groton, Connecticut

THE LORD IS MY SHEPHERD

for S.A.T.B. voices, a cappella

Psalm 23

ROBERT G. NEWTON

JESUS LEADS ME ALL THE WAY

for S.A.T.B. voices, a cappella

J. PAUL WILLIAMS
(ASCAP)

DAVID LANTZ III
(ASCAP)

Je - sus breaks through with His sun - shine, _____

cov - er all the land.   He

and He takes me by the hand, _____

breaks through with His sun - shine,   yes, He

17
(rejoin section)

takes me by the hand. Je - sus holds my hand, ___ yes He

commissioned for the Centennial Celebration
of the First Church of the Brethren, Harrisburg, Pennsylvania
in memory of Robert I. Hess,
who served the church faithfully as organist and member of the Christus Choir

WE ARE SURROUNDED

for S.A.T.B. voices, *a cappella*

Words by
J. PAUL WILLIAMS (ASCAP)
Based on Hebrews 12:1-3

Music by
JOSEPH M. MARTIN (BMI)

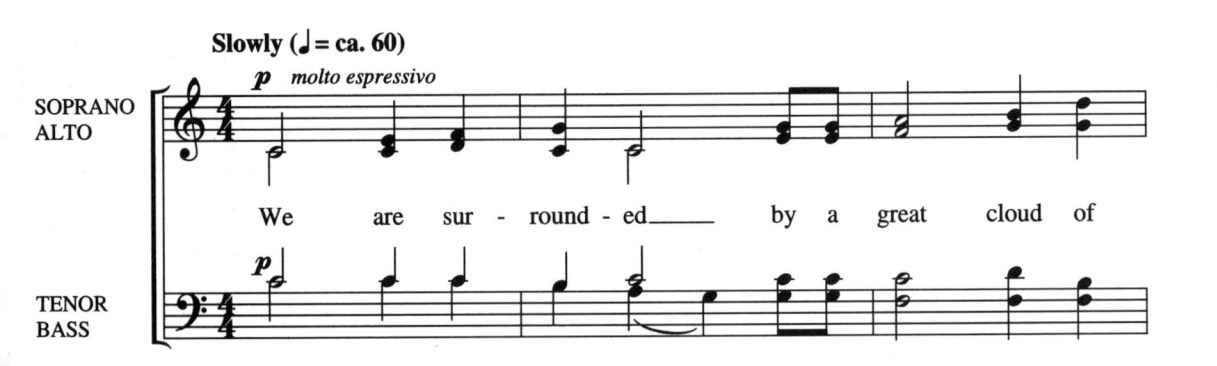

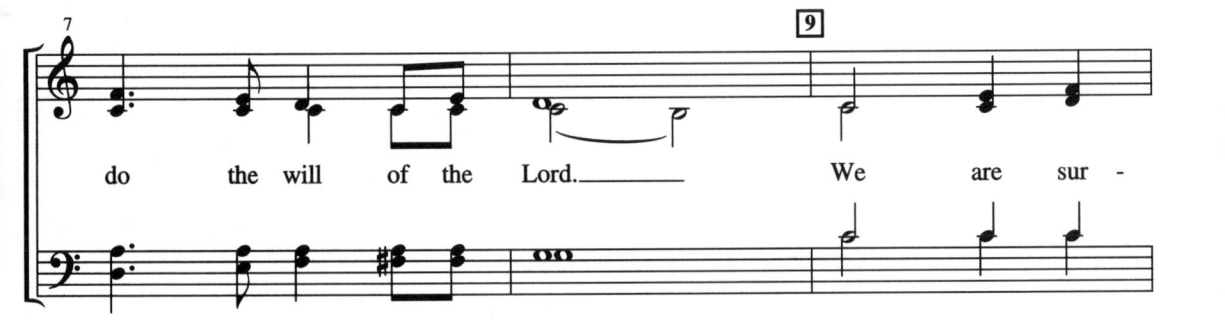

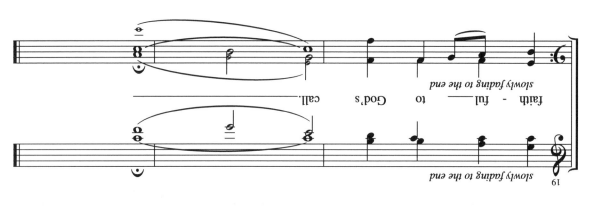

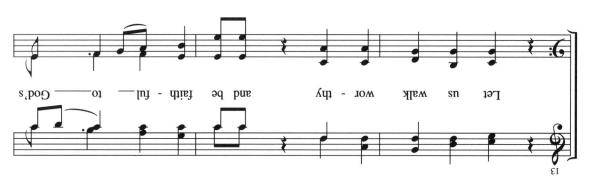

Great Joy A-Comin'!

for S.A.T.B. voices, unaccompanied

Words by
JOSEPH GRAHAM

Music by
DAVID ANGERMAN (ASCAP)
and JOSEPH GRAHAM (BMI)

* Close to final consonant.

34

* Close to final consonant.

ALL ON A STARRY NIGHT

for S.A.T.B. voices, a cappella

Words by
J. PAUL WILLIAMS (ASCAP)

Music by
JOSEPH GRAHAM (BMI)

42

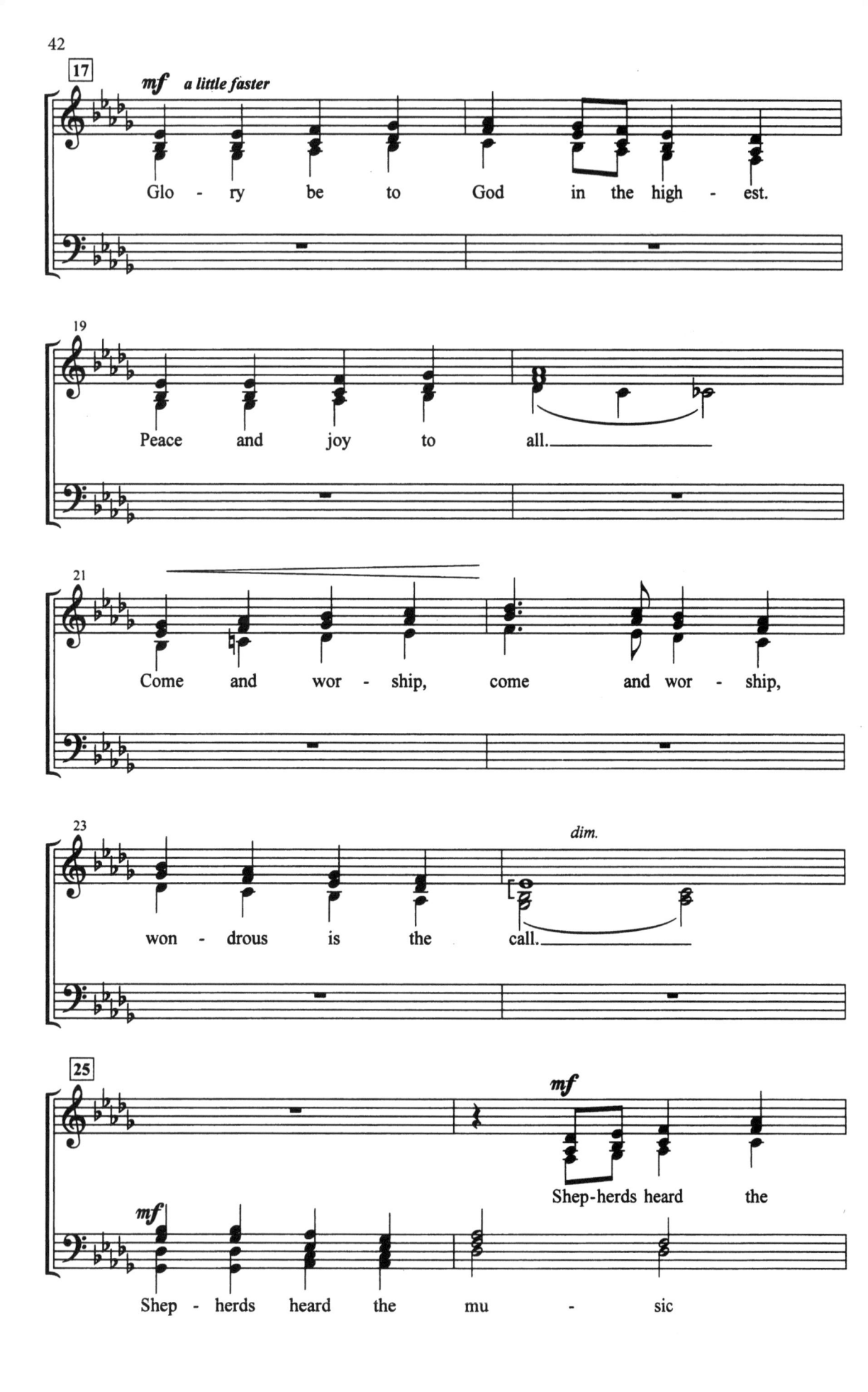

THE LIGHT OF THE WORLD!

for S.A.T.B. voices, a cappella

Words by DON BESIG
and NANCY PRICE (ASCAP)

Music by
DON BESIG (ASCAP)

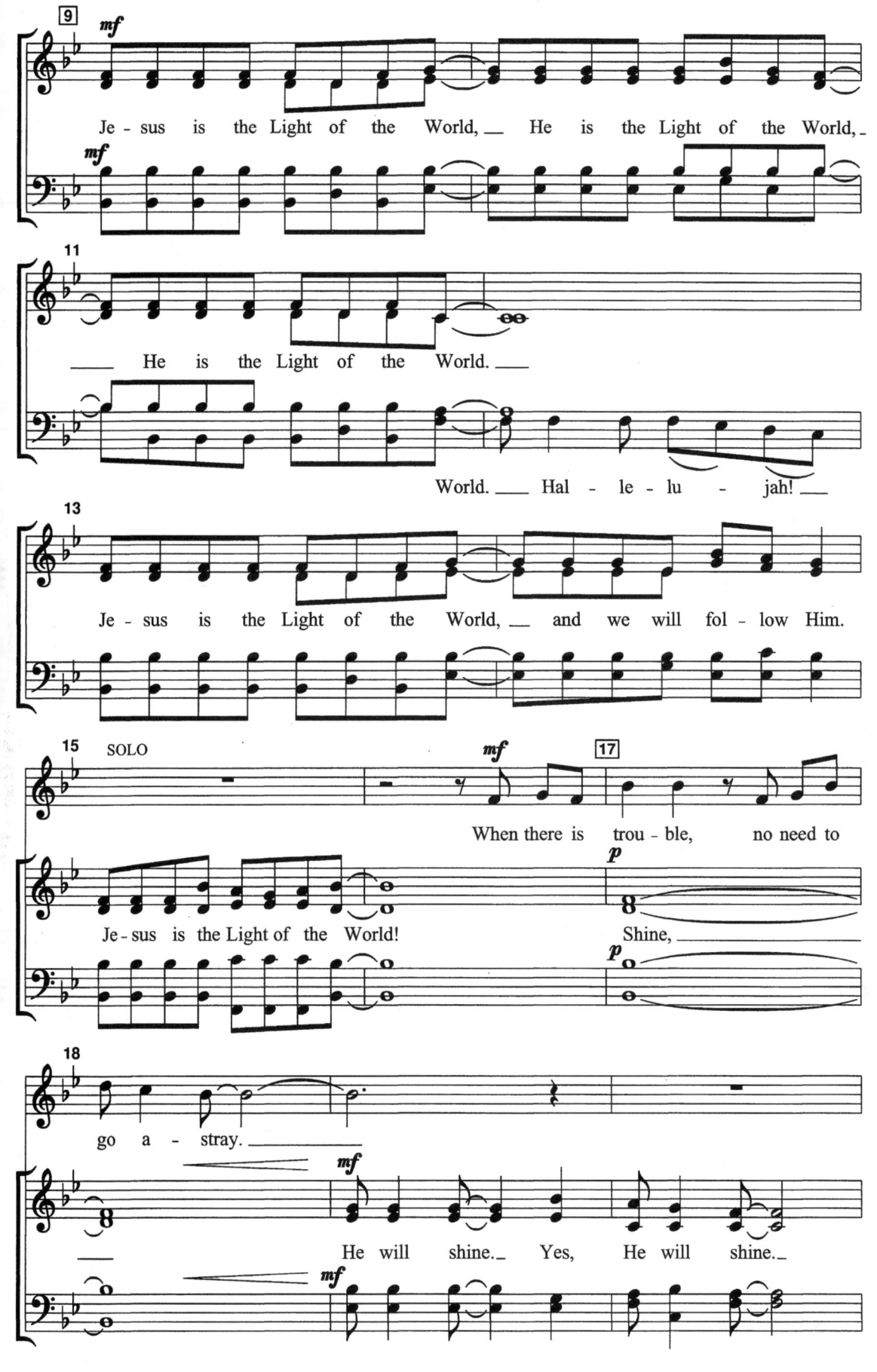

AMERICA, THE BEAUTIFUL

for S.A.T.B. voices with soprano solo,
unaccompanied

Words by
KATHERINE LEE BATES
Music by
SAMUEL A. WARD

Arranged by
ROY RINGWALD

Very moderately *(freely, as felt)*

grain, For pur - ple moun-tain maj - es -ties A - bove the fruit - ed

Hm

A - mer - i - ca! A - mer - i - ca! God shed His grace on

plain. A - mer - i - ca! A - mer - i - ca! God shed His grace on

* Dotted slur means no breath here.

** Divide men's voices into three equal parts (some 2nd Tenors singing 1st Bass).

13

thee, And crown thy good with broth - er-hood From sea to shin-ing sea.

thee,___ And crown thy good with broth - er-hood From sea to shining sea.

thee,___ And crown thy good with broth - er-hood From sea to shin-ing sea.

thee, And crown thy good with broth - er-hood From sea to shin-ing sea.

mp **18**

S. or A. SOLO

O beau - ti - ful for pil - grim feet Whose stern im - pas-sioned stress A

p legato

Hm___

p legato

Hm___

p legato

Hm___

p legato

Hm___ Hm___

18

p legato

for Brazeal Dennard and the Brazeal Dennard Chorale, Detroit, Mich.

Lord, I Believe In You
(Credo)

for S.A.T.B. voices, a cappella

GORDON YOUNG

62

MEDITATION FOR COMMUNION

for S.A.T.B. voices, a cappella

Words by
REGINALD HEBER (1783-1826)

Music by
JAY ALTHOUSE (ASCAP)

Performance time: approx. 1:20

sor - row bro - ken, Look on the tears by sin - ners___ shed;

And be the feast to us the to - ken, That by thy grace our

souls are ___ fed. Bread of the world in mer - cy bro - ken,

Wine of the soul in mer - cy shed. A - men, a - men.

In The Shadow Of The Cross

Words by
BARBARA FURMAN (BMI)

Music by
DAVID ANGERMAN (ASCAP)

WONDERFUL SAVIOR

for S.A.T.B. voices, a cappella

Words and Music by
ELISHA HOFFMAN (1839-1929)

Tune: BENTON HARBOR
Arranged by
JOSEPH GRAHAM (BMI)
and LEE SULLIVAN (ASCAP)

WE ARE NOT ALONE

for S.A.T.B. voices and optional solo, a cappella

Words and Music by
PEPPER CHOPLIN (ASCAP)

*Optional shaker may be used (e.g. egg shaker) beginning two measures before the choir and ending at the downbeat of m. 59. A constant eighth note pattern should be used.

*No breath.

48

we are nev-er a - lone.

we are nev-er a - lone, are not a-lone, we are not a-lone,

51

we are not a-lone, God is with us. We are not a-lone,

54

we are not a-lone, we are not a-lone, God is with us.

Our

57

God is with us now.

We are not a-lone, God is with us now.

RING YE BELLS OF EASTER MORNING

for S.A.T.B. voices, unaccompanied

Words by DON BESIG
and NANCY PRICE (ASCAP)

Music by
DON BESIG (ASCAP)

* Close to "ng" quickly.

* Close to "ng" quickly.

* Close to "ng" quickly.

* Do *not* close to "ng" here.

to the memory of Erik Routley, 1917-1982

My Master From A Garden Rose

for S.A.T.B. voices, unaccompanied

G. Y.

GORDON YOUNG

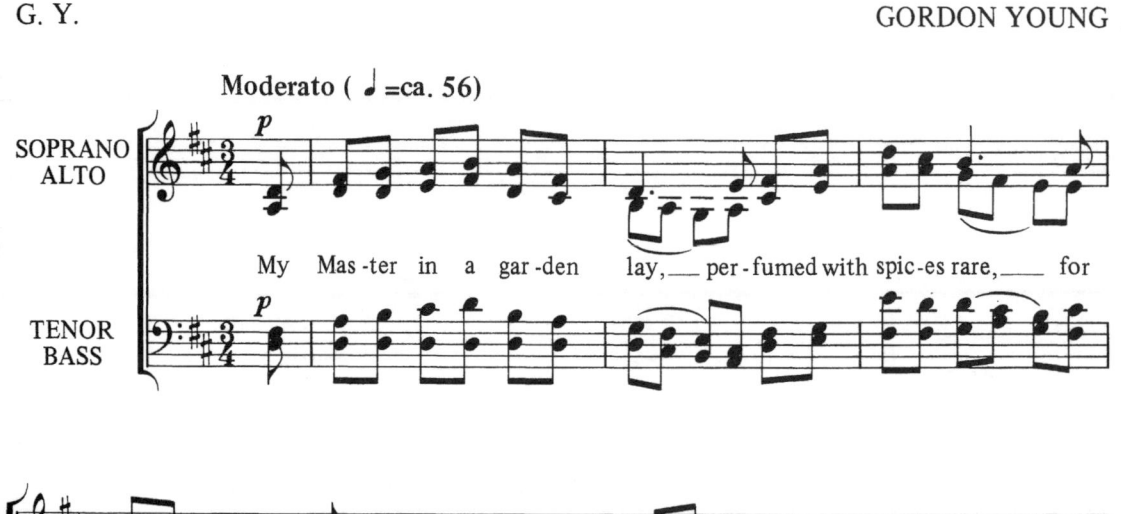

Performance time: approx. 1:45

A PARTING BLESSING

(for mixed voices, unaccompanied)

Traditional text

J. JEROME WILLIAMS

May the road rise to meet you; May the wind be al-ways at your back; May the sun shine warm up-on your face. May the rain fall soft up-on your fields; And un-til we meet a-gain, May God hold you in the palm of His hand.

Performance time: 1:45 (without extension: :50)
*Very slight break.

*Also available for S.A.B. (D–371), S.S.A. (B–529) and T.T.B.B. (C–250).

88

(OPTIONAL EXTENSION)
With more movement

Slower

*No breath here.